The Flag We Love

 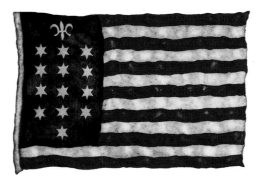 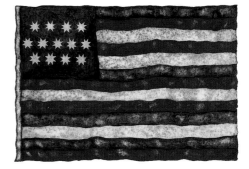

By **Pam Muñoz Ryan**

Illustrated by **Ralph Masiello**

 Charlesbridge

To my children: Marcy, Annie, Matthew, and Tyler
—P. R.

The author and illustrator thank
the National Aeronautics and Space Administration,
the Smithsonian Institution, the Byrd Polar Research Center,
the National Flag Foundation, and especially, Jerry Pallotta.

Published by
Charlesbridge Publishing
85 Main Street, Watertown, MA 02472
(617) 926-0329
www.charlesbridge.com

Printed in the United States of America
(hc) 20 19 18 17 16 15 14 13 12 11
(sc) 20 19 18 17 16 15 14 13 12 11 10 9 8 7 6
Printed on recycled paper

Library of Congress Cataloging-in-Publication Data
Ryan, Pam Muñoz.
    The flag we love / by Pam Muñoz Ryan;
illustrated by Ralph Masiello.
        p.   cm.
    ISBN 0-88106-845-4 (reinforced for library use)
    ISBN 0-88106-844-6 (softcover)
    1. Flags—United States—Juvenile literature.
[1. Flags.] I. Masiello, Ralph, ill. II. Title.
CR113.R93 1996
929.9'2'0973 — dc20   95-6619

In loving memory of my dad . . . a true artist, a great American.
— R. M.

Our flag is our country's symbol
Of ideals that are meant to last
It's a promise for our future
A reminder of our past.

The many connotations
For which our banner stands
Reflect our country's best intentions
And the people of this land.

A seamstress stitched a banner
For a country proud and new
From ribbonworks of red and white
And a yard of deep sky blue.

★ Who made the first Stars and Stripes? No one knows for sure. There are many stories and myths about its origin. Many historians consider Francis Hopkinson, one of the signers of the Declaration of Independence, to be the designer. Betsy Ross, a seamstress, did sew one of the earliest versions of the flag for the Pennsylvania Navy in 1777. As for who made the very first flag, it is still a mystery. ★ America's first flags had thirteen stars on a blue field and thirteen stripes to represent the thirteen colonies. At first, there were no guidelines about the arrangement of the stars and stripes, how big the blue field should be, or how many points the stars should have. Flagmakers were free to make many designs. ★

A teacher raises a radiant flag
To let the children know
The schoolyard is a place to come
For the chance to learn and grow.

★ The Stars and Stripes flew over a log schoolhouse as early as 1812 in Colrain, Massachusetts. ★ In the late 1800s, James B. Upham, a patriot, wanted schoolchildren to show love for their country. He asked them to save their pennies to buy American flags for their schools. His idea was popular with both children and adults, and within a year they raised enough money to purchase thousands of flags. ★ Today, as a patriotic custom, the flag is still flown near schools when classes are in session. ★

Americans stand together
Before ceremonies start
And promise their allegiance
With their hands across their hearts.

★ "I pledge allegiance to the flag of the United States of America and to the Republic for which it stands, one Nation under God, indivisible, with liberty and justice for all."
★ The original Pledge of Allegiance, written by Francis Bellamy, first appeared in a children's magazine in 1892. He wrote it to honor the 400th anniversary of Columbus's voyage to America. The following month, children first recited the pledge in public schools in celebration of Columbus Day. ★

The diligent Stars and Stripes waved on
Through the long and pounding night,
While patriots prayed that they would see
Their flag at morning's light.

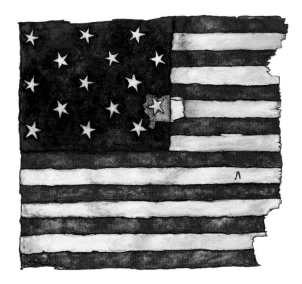

★ From a boat in Baltimore Harbor, Francis Scott Key observed the British bombing of Fort McHenry in the War of 1812. During the night, he saw only glimpses of the American flag through the smoke and flares of light. The next morning, he was so happy to see the flag still flying that he began writing a poem. Later, this poem was put to the tune of another song and became America's national anthem, "The Star-Spangled Banner." ★ The flag that inspired "The Star-Spangled Banner" was made by Mary Pickersgill and her daughter, Caroline. It measured thirty feet by forty-two feet. It was as wide as most two-story houses are tall! Today, that restored flag is on display at the Smithsonian Institution in Washington, D.C. ★

A casket draped with a solemn flag
Journeyed the countryside
While people came from town and field
To mourn the man who died.

★ While the flag is often flown during joyous occasions, it is also displayed at serious events. When President Lincoln was assassinated in 1865, his flag-draped casket was carried by train from Washington, D.C., to his family home in Springfield, Illinois.

★ When the flag is flown halfway down the flagpole, it is said to be flying at half-staff or half-mast. It is flown in this position to honor the memory of someone who has died. ★

Explorers carried a weary flag
Through snow and sun and wind
And left the banner on the spot
That marked their journey's end.

★ In 1926, Richard E. Byrd and his pilot, Floyd Bennett, were the first to fly over the North Pole. Three years later, after Bennett died, Byrd and three companions were the first to fly over the South Pole. Before that historic flight, Byrd took a stone from Bennett's gravesite and tied to it a small American flag. Then, as he flew over the South Pole, he dropped the flag and stone as a tribute to his ex-pilot and to all polar expeditions. ★ Explorers often plant flags when they reach their destinations to show that someone from their country has been there. ★

Children wave their festive flags
And parade along the way
As the drums roll and trumpets blare
The rhythms of the day.

★ On July 4, 1776, the original thirteen colonies declared their independence from Great Britain. This new United States of America adopted a constitution in 1787. The next year, on the fourth of July, the citizens of Philadelphia held a parade in celebration. Over the years, this practice continued. The Fourth of July, or Independence Day, has become a time for flags, parades, picnics, and fireworks. ★

Athletes strain to be the best
To the wild and thunderous roar
Of fans who chant their country's name
With hopes their team will score.

When people come to our great country
Aboard ships that cross the sea
They are welcomed to our harbors
By the flags of liberty.

★ Since 1942, the flag has been flown in all of America's ports of entry. It is one of the first things seen by people aboard ships. In this way, visitors from other lands and Americans returning home are welcomed by the symbol of freedom. ★ On land or at sea, when the flag is flown upside-down, it is considered a signal of emergency or distress. ★

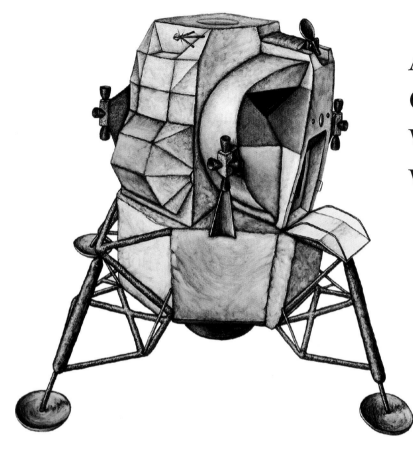

Astronauts planted a peaceful flag
On a far-off, distant world
Where it stands serene and silent
With the Stars and Stripes unfurled.

★ In 1969, Apollo 11 astronauts Neil Armstrong and Edwin Aldrin, Jr., landed on the moon in the lunar module, Eagle. On this historic journey, they took three American flags. One was planted on the moon, and the other two were brought back to earth and flown over the houses of Congress. Near the flag planted on the moon is a stainless-steel plaque that reads: "Here men from the planet Earth first set foot on the Moon. July 1969 A.D. We came in peace for all mankind." ★ Astronauts have planted American flags on the moon six times, one flag for each Apollo mission that landed there. ★

Heroes shoulder valiant flags
Twice, three times, and more
And claim the fronts of battlefields
On home and distant shores.

★ Many Americans have died fighting for our country and for the rights of people around the world. Many monuments have been built to commemorate these heroes, including the Vietnam Veterans Memorial in Washington, D.C. ★ Plaques and statues are placed in parks and near public buildings all over the country to honor our nation's heroes. People leave flags near monuments as a tribute to those they love. ★

Citizens march for freedom
With action, faith, and word.
A righteous banner guarantees
Their voices will be heard.

★ The government of the United States of America is based on democracy, or government by the people. The flag represents the peoples' rights to defend or protest a cause — to speak out about the things in which they believe. People often carry flags as a symbol of these rights. ★ The Latin words *E Pluribus Unum,* or "one out of many," appear on the Great Seal of the United States, which was designed as an emblem for the United States government. *E Pluribus Unum* means one nation made up of many states or one nation made up of many people. ★

A brilliant flag is shining
In a fireworks of light
While the people watch in wonderment
In the deepening, darkling night.

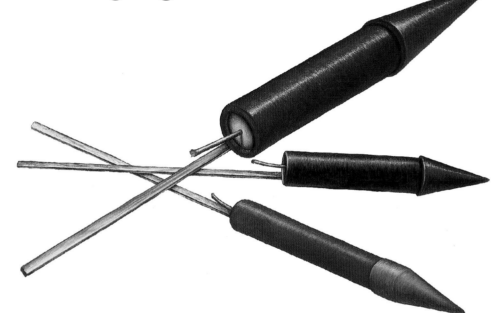

★ Communities celebrate national holidays with fireworks and patriotic music. On these occasions, Americans often feel a kinship with their fellow citizens and a loyalty to their country. ★ There is no official record of why red, white, and blue were chosen for the American flag. A resolution regarding the Great Seal of the United States defined the meanings of the country's colors several years after the flag was designed. Red stands for hardiness and courage, white for purity and innocence, and blue for vigilance, perseverance, and justice. ★

A citizen wears a symbol
A tiny, flag-shaped pin
As a promise for our future
And a reminder of where we've been.

★ People show their patriotism in many ways. They wear flag pins, display flags outside their homes, and participate in parades. When you see the American flag, remember that it does not represent one cause, but many causes; that it does not represent one person, but many people; and that it does not represent one ideal, but many of America's hopes and dreams. ★

Celebrate the flag we love
A majesty in the sky
And feel the pride that swells inside
As our banner goes streaming by.